# Lend a Hand

By Sue Graves

CELEBRATION PRESS
Pearson Learning Group

Why should you lend a hand?

**Why You Should Lend a Hand**
☺ To help someone

You can help someone.

You can learn new things.

Why You Should Lend a Hand
- ☺ To help someone
- ☺ To learn new things

You may feel grown-up.

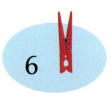

**Why You Should Lend a Hand**
☺ To help someone
☺ To learn new things
☺ To feel grown-up

How will you lend a hand?